Praise for 3 LINES 30 DAYS

"*Michele Marie Neyers' collection of poems takes the reader on an emotional journey through her compellingly deep and thought provoking expressions. Even if the reader has no intention of writing his or her own poems, this book is interesting and inspiring from a pure creativity mindset. We read, we imitate, and from this process we find our own voice and style. This is clearly a lady who has poured her heart out over what I assume must have been emotions and events she has experienced first-hand and shared in order to help us write our own story through poetry. I recommend this to anyone who enjoys poetry!*"

~ Peggy McColl – *New York Times* Best Selling Author

"*What a truly unique collection of poems! Each time I read the 3 lines of a poem, I was immediately drawn in and oftentimes found myself wanting more. It was like each poem had its own story, its own little mystery wrapped inside of it just waiting for the reader to experience and reveal it. Such a delightful book!*"

~ Judy O'Beirn – International Bestselling Author of
    Unwavering Strength

"*Michele takes the reader 'behind the scenes' and into the creative mind of a poet. I loved reading what brought the poems about in the first place. We all have an inner poet and Michele shows us how she taps in so we can do it too. Bravo!*"

~ Colleen Aynn – International Bestselling Author of the
    Feeling Friends series

"*Michele has learned to tap into the deep vein of creative energy that lives in all of us, crafting a life of intention where art and beauty are paramount. Her debut book of personal and insightful poetry is born from that same place. She is inviting us to indulge in our own muse as well, and we are all well served in accepting that invitation. The joy in discovering the merits of the journey she is asking us to take with her was real and unexpected. Come along!*"

~ Maulik Shah – Author of *Things To Teach My Daughters*,
    www.thingsmydaughters.com

3 LINES
30 DAYS

Unleash Your Inner Poet

"Poetry is the rhythmical creation of beauty in words."
Edgar Allan Poe

written by Michele Marie Neyers

Illustrations by Elin Maria Parmhed

Foreword by Melissa B Zeligman

Permission should be addressed in writing to Michele Marie Neyers at michele@micheleneyers.com

Cover Design: Michele Marie Neyers, michele@micheleneyers.com

Illustrations: Elin Maria Parmhed, elin@elinparmhed.com

Layout: Anne Karklins, annekarklins@gmail.com

ISBN-13: 978-1-989161-02-9

ISBN-10: 1989161022

Hasmark
PUBLISHING

This book is dedicated to my fellow peace walkers,
the Global Jam 4 Peace Ambassadors,
who bring their light and love into the world
through the universal language of music.

Foreword

"At the touch of love everyone becomes a poet."
~ Plato

I was trying to recall the exact moment that I first met Michele Marie Neyers. And while I cannot pin-point that moment, I do know that we knew about each other for months before we actually met. As often happens in the world of creatives and seekers, we shared many insightful, generous people in our social and creative circles. Our paths were destined to cross.

Above all, I fancy myself a writer. I like beginnings and endings. I like middles too, but I find births and deaths to be profound, sacred actually. I count the beginning of our friendship and our creative collaboration to be one of sacredness with no known foreseeable end in sight. I am honored and delighted to be writing the foreword of *3 Lines 30 Days – Unleash Your Inner Poet*.

I have always loved the poets. From those early childhood rhymes my mother read or sung to me, to my introductions to Rumi, Walt Whitman, Sylvia Plath, Hafiz, Mirabai, Mary Oliver, Diane Ackerman, Virginia Woolf and my guardian angel, Anais Nin. Growing up, I would hide out in the stacks of our local public library and devour pages of prose. As a young girl, I didn't always understand what the words meant but I noticed the sensations in my body and emotion that would arise and cling to me for days after reading something that moved me. I felt seen and understood by the poets. I've always had a deep desire and need for beauty in my world – created and natural. Especially the beauty of nature. The ocean has long served as a Muse and medicine in my life. When I'm away from it for a long period I ache for it. I miss it like I miss a lover. The reunion with the sea is an experience of being restored, rebirthed, returned. Beauty also presents in language. In our current ethos, it's one of the most accessible and reliable expressions of beauty I know. Songs, stories, love letters, social media posts and on and on. You get the picture, yes?

I started writing my own poetry in earnest in 2007 following an exquisite love affair. It was the birth of my truth and my vulnerability and the birth of **girl&muse**, my first creative platform for my poetry and art. Skip ahead several years to 2012 when I met the poet Michael K. Brown. Michael introduced me to the practice of writing three lines of poetry a day for 30 days. I was completely enamored with the concept and truth be told a little intimidated. I took on the practice for 30 days. What opened up for me was my ability to trust myself. Since that first exploration I've continued to take on the practice year after year. It has become essential to my creative process. I have never been a person that journals or keeps a diary. These three line missives over the years are as close as I have gotten. The practice serves as a biography of sorts where I can look back and recall what was happening and who was in my world at that time. It has provided friends and fellow creatives a glimpse into my life and for some has offered connection and inspiration.

Early in our friendship over good food, great bourbon and even greater conversations, Michele and I shared about our passion for writing. We both had a commitment to making a difference in the world and forwarding the expression of the feminine voice. I encouraged her to take on writing three lines of poetry for 30 days as an access to her greater mission and to fulfill her own creative cravings. It obviously struck a chord. The stunning book you hold in your hands is her start, her beginning. I invite you to dwell in each line. To seek and discover a new facet of yourself and life. Let it spark your own creativity and consider saying "YES!" to the challenge she puts forth.

We may never know who started poetry, but I want to acknowledge Michael K. Brown for introducing this practice to me and Michele for bringing it to the world.

With love, Melissa B Zeligman

DAY 31 | JANUARY 31, 2017

We need our artists and lovers now.
Our seekers, wanderers and touchstones.
Where language fails, art transcends.

Melissa B Zeligman

Author's Notes

This book contains my original poetry and is organized into three distinct collections. Collection 1 and 2 inspired the title of this book – *3 LINES 30 DAYS*. The Special Collection is a handful of poems selected from my personal journals. Each of the collections reflects a particular path and timeframe on my journey of discovery and awakening.

Collection 1 – Summer 2013 | The first collection was written during the warm summer months here in the mid-Atlantic region of the United States. I was enjoying my second summer season at the dream home I had designed and built on the water. So many new things to explore! Many of the poems written during this time were about love, transformation, spirituality, and sensuality.

Collection 2 – Winter 2017 | Inspired once again to pick up my pen and do another 30-day challenge, this second collection was written nearly four years later and during a different season of the year and my life. The poems in this collection reflect a renewed love for music, being in love, spreading the message of peace and hope, and the awesomeness of life. One of the 'subtle' differences in this collection is that each poem was given a title, sometimes after it was written and sometimes before.

Special Collection | The third and final collection contains a handful of poems written during what I like to call the 'in-between times'. Those times of thoughtful reflection, spontaneous creativity, and when the burning desire to express something is too strong to ignore.

About the 3 Lines 30 Days Poetry Challenge | In 2013, I was introduced to a simple poetry challenge. Essentially the challenge put before me was this – write 3 lines of poetry every day for 30 days in a row. The poems didn't have to rhyme or follow a predetermined format. There were no complicated rules nor was there a requirement to share what I'd written with anyone.

Being a woman who doesn't like to follow the rules or have people tell her what to do or how to do it, I can tell you that the 30-day challenge resonated with every fiber of my being. That doesn't mean I believed I could actually do it. Not at first. I still had some old programming that needed to be overwritten. You see, I didn't really 'see' myself as a poet. I'd always thought about poets as being extremely gifted and intellectually superior. As compared to myself, that is. Wasn't poetry supposed to be complicated and complex?

What I didn't know at the time – that I now know to be true – is that the age-old saying "I'll believe it when I see it" is all wrong. The truth is that you have to believe something in order to see it. Believe that you are already a poet, and it will be expressed in your reality. The 'believing' comes first in that universal equation. Frankly, sometimes our beliefs need a good boost or kick in the pants before we begin to see something even close to what we want. As I progressed through the challenge, one day at a time, I began to believe. Each day my belief in myself as a poet and a writer grew stronger. And then my belief grew more as I began to share my poems with others. And it grew even more still when I completed the 30-day challenge a second and third time.

This challenge is intentionally designed to be simple. But don't let its simplicity fool you. You may be surprised, even delighted, by what happens when you make a commitment to do the challenge for 30 days. I found that words just started flow, like a faucet that just keeps pouring water from its spout. And the words would oftentimes flow at the most inconvenient of times – while driving, brushing my teeth, or out for a walk. Oftentimes it would simply start with a word or two, or maybe even a whole phrase.

My advice to you is this: Just let it flow the way it is meant to flow. Don't force it. Be aware of the inspiration surrounding you at all times. Don't prejudge what comes up for you to write about. Follow that instinct, that intuition that only YOU have.

Follow that intuition. Surrender to it. Trust that the words will always spill forth when they are ready to do so. Because they are always and already there.

Details on how to participate in the *3 LINES 30 DAYS* poetry challenge can be found at: www.3lines30days.com. I'd love to personally hear how the 30-day challenge goes for you! Write to me anytime at michele@ micheleneyers.com.

Table of Contents

Introduction

I f asked to describe the intention behind this book in 3 words or less, here's what I would say: Poetry, Beauty and Creativity. The three things I hold most dear, that resonate at the heart-center and deepest depths of me. Something that many of my closest friends and mentors know about me is my passion and utter obsession for all things beautiful + useful. If it's not beautiful AND useful, I have no interest in creating it, wearing it, using it, buying it … you get the picture! This book is a living, breathing expression of that passion and has been designed in such a way where I can share with you a collection of beautiful + original poetry and offer you a fun + very useful creativity challenge all in one fell swoop-ty swoop! My musings on Poetry, Beauty and Creativity follow here.

On Poetry | If music is the language of the Soul, then poetry is the food that nourishes the Soul. Poetry is the barque on which the Soul is taken on a journey and then comes back to rest upon itself having been transformed forever.

A song is poetry {lyrics} put to music. The already lyrical nature of poetry weds itself nicely to the rhythms and vibrations of music. What you experience as you read a work of poetry or listen to a song is the energetic vibrations, the frequencies that the writers, the poets, the musicians have all embedded and infused into their creations. We feel the "emotions" that they have felt being evoked in us through their soul-stirring words. There is a transference of that energy to us and we are able to "feel" and experience those intended emotions within our own physical being.

This is a wonderful and truly powerful thing! It is why certain song lyrics and music stay with you for a very long time. It is why when you hear those words or music again – even after a very long time – you can relive the emotions you had when you first heard them. That transference that happens occurs between the words / music and your "emotional" (subconscious) mind. Here it is planted and here it remains.

"Poetry is the rhythmical creation of beauty in words."
~ Edgar Allan Poe

On Beauty | Beauty is everywhere, and it is in everything. It is around us and ever present at all times. But so often Beauty can go unnoticed or unappreciated. Have you ever noticed the power Beauty has to stop you in your tracks? Perhaps you couldn't take your eyes off a sunset that cascaded an array of orange, pink and purple ribbons across the sky. Or you wonder if anyone else noticed that lone red rose lying haphazardly in an airport breezeway, having gotten accidentally separated from its original bouquet. What about that gorgeous ceramic pot sitting in your garage that is just waiting for someone to notice its potential as a home for a beautiful cluster of succulents.

The truth is that only our awareness of Beauty will cause Her to rise up to greet us. Yes, let me say that one more time. Only our belief and awareness of Beauty will cause something to be Beautiful.

Beauty asks us to simply be fully aware of Her and to believe in Her existence. She will ask us to stop and appreciate that sunset on our drive home from work or to pick up that lone red rose and take a sweet whiff of its soft fragrance. She may even inspire us to bring flowers for our loved one when we arrive home at the end of the day. The desire we hold for Beauty and our expectancy for it to exist will call Her out from behind the shadows. She wants more than anything to be seen and to be celebrated. She is for full self-expression and expansion. Like a moth being drawn by a flame, we can attract to us the Beauty that we wish to see and experience in the world around us.

"What is etched in our hearts, we can hold in our hands."

On Creativity | I am always the first to correct someone I hear say something like "I am not creative" or "I could never write poetry". Each one of us has the power of Divine Intelligence that comes to and through us at all times. With that Divine Intelligence comes our power to create. We are each of us creators. We need only be aware of this truth and believe in our creative powers.

In James Allen's well-known book 'As A Man Thinketh', the author includes an original poem at the end of Chapter 2 – *Effect of Thought on Circumstances*. To me this poem speaks volumes about our innate creative power as human beings.

You will be what you will to be;
Let failure find its false content
In that poor word, "environment".
But spirit scorns it and is free.

It masters time, it conquers space;
It cows that boastful trickster, Chance.
And bids the tyrant Circumstance
Uncrown, and fill a servant's place.

The human Will, that force unseen.
The offspring of a deathless Soul.
Can hew a way to any goal,
Though walls of granite intervene.

Be not impatient in delay,
But wait as one who understands:
When spirit rises and commands,
The gods are ready to obey.

Collection 1 – Summer 2013

3 LINES 30 DAYS | DAY 1 | AUGUST 1, 2013

The erotic creature within,
An enchanting goddess flowing and free,
Longs for her ultimate unleashing.

To be someone's deepest desire,
All of her exposed in a delicious exploration for joy and pleasure.

Her heart in blissful union with His heals them both.

3 LINES 30 DAYS | DAY 2 | AUGUST 2, 2013

What magic is this that releases a longing held captive?

Like a love-tipped arrow,
Your words pierced clean through
To its intended target.

Dead inside crying out for help in silence
Until you spoke and I saw myself in you
Like a perfect divine reflection.

3 LINES 30 DAYS | DAY 3 | AUGUST 3, 2013

Awake and asleep,
Our naked bodies side by side,
I am distracted by my desire to touch you.

I reach out to caress your peaceful face.

Your breath catches for just a moment
And then returns to a steady rhythm
To which my heart smiles with such sweet love.

3 LINES 30 DAYS | DAY 4 | AUGUST 4, 2013

My body finds rest in a desert oasis
That caresses its contours with gentle care.

Nature gives over its solitude to my soul.

Our bodies are but a perilous and temporary
Bridge between nature and spirit,
Life as we know it
Hanging
Between two undeniably powerful forces.

3 LINES 30 DAYS | DAY 5 | AUGUST 5, 2013

Awakening to a new day filled with possibilities,
Her tender feet swing down to touch the chilled floor.

Her thoughts wander to dreams
That easily remind her of her desires.

She experiences her insignificance
And her magnificence
Wash over her all at once.

Oil-stained fingers, sweat and grime …
The markings of a hard-working man
Comes strutting through my door.

As one of your strong arms slips slowly
Around my waist and draws me in,
Heartbeats synchronize to a common rhythm.

Instantly I am safe inside your embrace.

3 LINES 30 DAYS | DAY 7 | AUGUST 7, 2013

Tell me where your desire lives.

Let the wildness in
And hear the voices deep inside you
Whispering your heart's truth.

Listen and follow the signs
As if your very life depended on it.

3 LINES 30 DAYS | DAY 8 | AUGUST 8, 2013

The smooth glide of a hand
Over a generously oiled mound
Awakens my desire.

Your breath synchronizes with mine
As the ancient dance of arousal begins.

Settling in we await the sweetest,
Most powerful release.

3 LINES 30 DAYS | DAY 9 | AUGUST 9, 2013

Silence and solitude act as my companion and teacher.

Physical, emotional, intellectual, spiritual …
Four dimensions of intimacy dance inside
Mutual self-revelation.

Discovery and rediscovery
Lie at the heart of its ultimate undoing.

3 LINES 30 DAYS | DAY 10 | AUGUST 10, 2013

You are not a puzzle to be solved
But a mystery to be lavishly enjoyed.

I am a rare soul
Opening my arms wide,
Embracing the joy of loving you and being loved.

I am the best version of myself
When you love me.

3 LINES 30 DAYS | DAY 11 | AUGUST 11, 2013

Deep inside our hearts do we hold
Our essential being and light.

Existing within those chambers is a soft quiet voice
That promises us a joyous reunion
With our eternal truth and divinity.

Will you be still long enough to listen?

3 LINES 30 DAYS | DAY 12 | AUGUST 12, 2013

Lost to this worldly plane too soon
We grieve for those we can no longer hold and love still.

Hearts broken, sometimes savagely
Ripped apart for no good reason.

Love one another always
For the experience of love
Is the fiercest healer.

3 LINES 30 DAYS | DAY 13 | AUGUST 13, 2013

There is something you should know about me.

When I chose to love you,
It means I will never stop.

I will always have your back
No matter what.

3 LINES 30 DAYS | DAY 14 | AUGUST 14, 2013

My heart is full of tiny wishes for you.

May you create happiness exactly where you are
In every moment.

And when happiness doesn't seem possible,
Create the possibility of happiness and remember
That everything we say, do, have and be
Is exactly how we create it.

3 LINES 30 DAYS | DAY 15 | AUGUST 15, 2013

Your finger moves across and around
My soft pink opening.

Swirling and teasing, slowly purposefully plunging
Between the wet folds
Gliding gently up over my engorged clit.

A pattern repeats as pleasure builds
And my body responds to the familiar rhythm of arousal.

3 LINES 30 DAYS | DAY 16 | AUGUST 16, 2013

Tension is building with every lap of your
Fingers and tongue around my pink lips.

Instinctually you know
When to apply pressure I so desperately need
As your fingers fuck me furiously.

You grab and twist both my nipples,
Shaking them to match the
Fire-stoking intensity now burning below.

3 LINES 30 DAYS | DAY 17 | AUGUST 17, 2013

I inhale deeply as the first waves of ecstasy
Begin to form and roll towards one another.

Exhaling slowly, I can feel those waves of sexual energy
Travel in and out of every molecule of my being.

Mmmmm … my entire body hums
To pleasure's beautiful symphony
Until I finally surrender
To my orgasm's ultimate release.

3 LINES 30 DAYS | DAY 18 | AUGUST 18, 2013

Your strong solid arms wrap around me
To hold my body close,
Yet your love stays at a safe distance.

When I am at my most vulnerable,
I also catch glimpses of your heart
Reaching out from inside its protective cage.

Have no fear, my love …
Unlock the cage with hope
And release your heart to be loved by mine.

3 LINES 30 DAYS | DAY 19 | AUGUST 19, 2013

Thoughts racing and heart thumping,
I take three deep healing breaths
To invoke the calm.

I close my eyes to the silence.

I am present
To the miracles of love and life.

3 LINES 30 DAYS | DAY 20 | AUGUST 20, 2013

Let go of the ties and hurts that bind you to the past
And embrace the new day before you.

Create with fresh eyes and an open heart.

Beauty and magic await
Those who believe in miracles.

3 LINES 30 DAYS | DAY 21 | AUGUST 21, 2013

Hello, do you know me?

I am your safe harbor in life's most wicked storms,
A fierce stand for the presence of
Love and joy in every moment.

My deepest desire is simply
To be known by you.

3 LINES 30 DAYS | DAY 22 | AUGUST 22, 2013

Do you see the beauty and divinity in one another?

Look not with your eyes but
With your own essence
And see the spirits walking around in physical form around you.

Each one of us
Is pure love and pure spirit.

3 LINES 30 DAYS | DAY 23 | AUGUST 23, 2013

I am an emerging Queen
Waiting for her loyal King.

He makes his appearance in my
Loveliest dreams of awakening.

He is my champion for a lifetime.

3 LINES 30 DAYS | DAY 24 | AUGUST 24, 2013

I hear you say the words 'I love you'
And know it to be true in my heart.

Love is an action word,
Hopeful and courageous.

I'm standing up to fight
For a lifetime of love and partnership …
Will you stand there with me?

3 LINES 30 DAYS | DAY 25 | AUGUST 25, 2013

Pleasure is creative, innocent, playful.

It is everywhere you are willing to look for it.

Go ahead …
Tune in to what pleases you.

3 LINES 30 DAYS | DAY 26 | AUGUST 26, 2013

Use the soul as your reference point and guide post.

Come back to it
For self-assurance and validation.

It is the true home
Of pure love and acceptance.

Michele Marie Neyers

3 LINES 30 DAYS | DAY 27 | AUGUST 27, 2013

Relinquish the 'I' in all your relationships.

Open the gates of your heart to sacred love.

Unconditionally radiate love
Like beams of sunshine
Out to the world.

3 LINES 30 DAYS | DAY 28 | AUGUST 28, 2013

Unhelpful labels and ancient attitudes about sexuality
Sadden me greatly.

Will it take generations to change it
Or can we have more meaningful dialogue
To speed up that change?

I see a time where sex is celebrated
As a magnificent and simple joy
Of our human experience.

3 LINES 30 DAYS | DAY 29 | AUGUST 29, 2013

Be patient all you heroes and goddesses.

The thought must be formed, the idea spoken,
The seed planted and the seedling loved
To fulfill on a dream as big as yours.

The time is sooner than you realize.

3 LINES 30 DAYS | DAY 30 | AUGUST 30, 2013

Sunshine on my face and bare shoulders.

Sand under my feet and between my toes.

Angels and blessings and dragonflies
Swirling all around me today.

Collection 2 – Winter 2017

BEAUTIFUL SOUL | DAY 1 | JANUARY 1, 2017

Beautiful soul, come whisper in my ear
Your most desperate longing and your fiercest desire.

Let the cage door swing open and your heart find liberation
In the hands of hope's rescue.

Lest you forget, even your deepest wounds
Experience perfect healing by the salves of time and love.

TURNING | DAY 2 | JANUARY 2, 2017

Turning leaves
Nature's signal for slowing down
And the promise
Of Spring's transformation.

Turning towards the pending darkness
In a moment of surrender
Accepting all that is
And all that is not.

Turning inwards
I reflect, renew
And come home to myself.

IF | DAY 3 | JANUARY 3, 2017

If you knew the depth of this love I have for you
That has grown and blossomed over time,
Would you draw closer to me
Or pull further away?

If you knew the expansiveness
Of the joy I feel in your presence
Would you embrace me fully
Or deny us both?

If you only knew, my sweet love
Could we be together
Now and forever?

ONLY LOVE | DAY 4 | JANUARY 4, 2017

In all directions, in all dimensions,
And in all of time
There has been only love.

To the ends of the earth
Through the dawning of the ages of ages
Only love.

Vanquish now
And let go of
Anything that is not love.

BODY BEAUTIFUL | DAY 5 | JANUARY 5, 2017

Feet first, then hips wade in,
Followed by arms and orbs floating atop the churning water.

A domed sky sparkles of amethyst stones,
While a chilly arctic igloo awaits nearby.

Carefully and intentionally I come peacefully to stillness
In a marbled sea of warm red clay.

WINTER WONDERLAND | DAY 6 | JANUARY 6, 2017

Fluffy snowflakes fall sideways
Outside my kitchen window
Painting a blanket of white
Across the landscape.

Soon I will hear the familiar sounds
Of rumbling snowplows and shovels
Scraping their metal tongues against concrete driveways.

For now I will snuggle under warm covers
Slip on my thickest and wooliest socks
Sip a steamy cup of chocolatey mocha goodness
While I watch this Winter Wonderland arrive on the scene.

CHANGE | DAY 7 | JANUARY 7, 2017

Sometimes change comes to us quietly over time,
Found in the moments of our day,
Through the viewing of milestones and markers along the way.

Sometimes change moves swiftly and without warning,
Pushing the breath from our lungs
And pulling the ground from underneath our feet.

And yet all change is necessary and wanted,
Inevitable for the evolution and growth we seek;
For you and for me and what is to come.

NOT ALONE | DAY 8 | JANUARY 8, 2017

If you've ever laughed
Simply because someone else was laughing,
You know how infectious laughter can be.

And do you also find
That a person expressing
Their passion and enthusiasm
For what it is they most care about
Can be twice as contagious?

Breathe fiery passion and full belly laughter
Into your own life, my friends,
And remember you can borrow from others
When you need to.

BEAUTIFUL + USEFUL | DAY 9 | JANUARY 9, 2017

Have nothing in your life and surroundings
That you do not know to be useful or believe to be beautiful.

Devoted am I to creating that which is both beautiful + useful
To support us in carrying out
The most delectable, juicy, deliberately conscious
And sustainable lives that we can imagine.

Always remember that you are so beautiful in every way,
Full of purpose and God's sacred promise.

UNVEILED | DAY 10 | JANUARY 10, 2017

Hearts open, open, open and open just a little bit more;
Each word we express turns a key that unlocks truth's door.

Pain, uncertainty, doubt, darkness, shadows, vulnerability, respect,
Appreciation, peace and love;
All of it revealed, revered and accepted.

I see you and you see me, unveiled.

MOON | DAY 11 | JANUARY 11, 2017

Full and voluptuous,
You lay claim to the wintry starry sky.

Bathe my bedroom in your glistening glow-y white splendor.

Shower down on me your healing energies;
Your luminous presence comforts me.

FINDING MY VOICE | DAY 12 | JANUARY 12, 2017

Somewhere along this long and winding road called life
You were lost to me;
Silenced, shunned and shushed
One too many times.

Oh, sweet and sexy warrior goddess,
When was it you decided
You had nothing important to say?

Your most beautiful instrument
Has been here all along
Waiting for you to sing the songs
That only exist inside YOU.

STRINGS | DAY 13 | JANUARY 13, 2017

Fingertips pressing down,
The sting of the pressure immediate, then suddenly fleeting.

Up and down, lift and shift,
Curled fingers dance over your silkiness again and again.

Strumming, humming, frets buzzing;
Then blissful harmonious synchronization.

BLESSINGS | DAY 14 | JANUARY 14, 2017

Simple yet so profound
Weekly wisdom
And sacred sisterhood shared.

Hearts wide open
Dreams envisioned
And then boldly declared;
Creating lives that we love.

The space, the gorgeous opening
And generous listening for what's possible;
My eternal gratitude
For the blessing you are in my life.

BOLDNESS | DAY 15 | JANUARY 15, 2017

Breathe boldness into your bones
And pump music into your veins.

Revive those passions you let die on the vine
So that you could become a 'grown up'.

Burn down the walls and wash away the ashes;
Today, and every day, wake up to LIFE.

DOMESTIC GODDESS | DAY 16 | JANUARY 16, 2017

Some say that to wear the coveted crown of the domestic goddess
Takes many a heroic effort.

No matter the size of your castle
Or the length of your to clean-launder-scrub-dust list,
This title is well within your reach by taking one easy step.

Your kingdom, Your rules;
Simply say 'I am a domestic goddess' and it is done!

GRATITUDES | DAY 17 | JANUARY 17, 2017

A glass container,
Little slips of paper and colorful pens.

A gracious, grateful moment captured in time and space;
Embellish with stickers if you wish.

Collect your gratitude as you go;
Open and revisit them as often as needed
To remember what a precious gift YOUR life truly is.

MERMAIDS | DAY 18 | JANUARY 18, 2017

Gazing into your aquamarine depths
I catch a glimpse of the starry-eyed girl I once was and still am.

With scales, a tail and a Rapunzel-like mane of blonde hair
Flowing past my waist.

The ocean is filled with beautiful dreams
And treasures left by mermaids.

TRANSITIONS | DAY 19 | JANUARY 19, 2017

Changing of the guard;
The pomp, circumstance and pageantry.

Let peace, unity and freedom for all
Sing out and ring out across the land.

Praying for change and
Ready for action fueled by love.

CHOICE | DAY 20 | JANUARY 20, 2017*

Back and forth
Tossing and turning
Struggling and debating;
Rinse and repeat.

Ask yourself the question:
What is the expression of your authentic Self,
The one that knows no attachments
And speaks the truest truth for you?

The choice is mine
And it is yours
Today I choose not to march.

Poet's Personal Note: There is SO much more to say here, about my inner struggle and ultimately my choice not to participate in the Women's March on Washington that weekend. I fully honor, love and appreciate all those who participated in DC and in cities across the country and around the world. Our authentic self-expression and voices are needed now more than ever ... keep standing and speaking up for what is true for you. Be the change you wish to see in the world.

ILLUMINATION | DAY 21 | JANUARY 21, 2017

Oh, whispers of wisdom,
Seek and ye shall find.

Shine brightly a light into the
Deep, dark corners of our world and ourselves.

Shadows, stand aside to make way
For a new beginning and a different path.

SPACE | DAY 22 | JANUARY 22, 2017

Do you see
The beauty and the Divinity
In one another?

Look not with your eyes
But with your own essence
And see the spirits walking and waking
In physical form all around you.

Each one of us
Is pure love
And pure spirit.

QUIET FIRES | DAY 23 | JANUARY 23, 2017

Quiet fires are burning,
The subtle winds that touch all leaves are stirring.

Play and creativity make for shifting perspectives.

Be open to deviating
From your one, perfect plan.

LET ME | DAY 24 | JANUARY 24, 2017

Let me seek first to understand;
Your path is yours and unknown to me.

Let me be patient and kind,
Spreading small acts of mercy
To ease another's suffering.

Let me be an instrument of love and peace,
A channel for healing and grace.

MINDFULNESS | DAY 25 | JANUARY 25, 2017

Mindfulness practiced in daily life
Holds the treasure we seek.

Thinking, fantasizing, hearing and feeling;
Noting the diversity of our experiences.

Exquisite moments, wide awake.

LOVE NOTES | DAY 26 | JANUARY 26, 2017

The music's inside of me
And it's inside of you.

Your unique energetic vibration
Serves the world
Like only you can.

Sing more love songs
Write more love notes
Erupt with the sounds of love!

Michele Marie Neyers

LUNA | DAY 27 | JANUARY 27, 2017

Curvy and petite, you are my perfect fit.

Beautiful and sensuous,
Words would fail to evoke the joy you evoke in me.

Sweet lady, let us create magic together at once.

PERSPECTIVE | DAY 28 | JANUARY 28, 2017

Shake up your habits, rattle your patterns.

Is it a 6 or a 9; a smooth cup or a cup with a handle?

Change your perspective, adjust your angle,
Look through another lens.

TAPESTRY | DAY 29 | JANUARY 29, 2017

Ideas and dialogue weave together;
The promise of a diverse and devoted tapestry.

Over and under, looping and locking;
Pull and stretch to bond and tighten.

Stronger as a whole than alone and apart, divided.

BEGINNINGS | DAY 30 | JANUARY 30, 2017

Endings mark the beginning
Of something new.

Sunsets will pass
Only to be followed
By even more glorious sunrises.

Where will my muse take me
And what grand adventures
Will we have next?

Special Collection

I DREAM OF YOU | MAY 20, 2017

I dream of you
Standing with me on a beach
Embracing, touching
Our faces illuminated by the
Full moon above
The warm glow of our campfire

I dream of you
Walking with me down that sandy beach
Hand in hand, fingers playing
Walking with me
Down the dusty, sunny paths of life

I dream of you
Lying with me under the stars
Dreaming dreams of peace, love & forever
Sharing, caring, supporting & laughing

I dream of you
Of you + me
Of starry nights
Joy-filled days
In love with Love
In love with Life

THE KEY OF LOVE | JUNE 20, 2017

Music in the key of love
Awakens my heart
Passions intertwine
Yours and mine
Sharps and flats
Notes fly off the page
Soaring to heights unseen
Music speaks in us all
Peace triumphs
Love conquers all

MORNING GRATITUDE | JUNE 29, 2017

I awake from my slumber
Finding you there
Waiting for me to play you
Strings strumming
To my heart frequency
Vibrations + palpitations
A language all its own
Universal is its reach
My heart smiles
The ultimate container
For precious memories
And those emotions
Long forgotten
Never gone

IF YOU ONLY KNEW | JULY 14, 2015

If you only knew
The dream on my heart
Reveals itself
As that of a circle
Illustrating unity and partnership
An infinite sea of possibilities

If you only knew
The song in my heart
Is that of a siren mermaid
Singing true love's tune
About a true & forever love

The sort of tune
That makes whiskey drinking cowboys cry
Proper ladies swoon
Playing on an endless loop
Sending ripples across galaxies
Waves over moon & stars

If you only knew
The beat of my heart
Beats in search of its
Beautiful harmonic equal
Brought together in purpose
Bound together in
Delicious partnership
And juicy consciousness

If you only knew
The dream on my heart is you.

REWARD | JULY 21, 2017

Our reward
For good-feeling thoughts
Mixed with a burning desire
Stirred up with feeling and emotions
Washed in persistence and repetition
Is we feel good
We feel fucking fantastic!

Love and Gratitude

This is something I know for sure. That none of us goes through our time on this earthly plane without impacting and influencing people we encounter along the way. I would never presume that I could acknowledge and thank ALL the people who have impacted and influenced me on my path. What I can and will do here is send out my heartfelt love and gratitude to those who have supported and encouraged me in the creation and birthing of this little beauty!

~

To my mentor Peggy McColl for the tireless encouragement and inspiration you give to aspiring and best-selling authors everywhere. You've helped pave the way for so many of us to realize the dream of becoming a successful published author and so much more! From the very moment we met at the August 2017 PGI Matrixx event, I knew I had finally found the path that would lead me to my destiny. You are a rare, authentic gem that shines bright and I appreciate you so much!

To Judy O'Beirn, Jenn Gibson, Anne Karklins and the entire team of "book fairies" at Hasmark Publishing – my eternal gratitude to each and every one of you for your expertise and close attention to every detail. I felt so taken care of in your capable and caring hands.

To my family for all the love and support you've always shown to me, not only with the birthing of this book but in everything I've ever done. To my two beautiful nieces, Michaela and Jenna, and my goddaughter, Sonja, who inspire me and who I always hope to inspire by living example.

To my circle of chosen sisters and women in my life who support me in countless ways to express the highest and best version of myself each and every day. You inspire me endlessly with your devotion, persistence, generosity, and love for all that is. I feel so fortunate to be among you for a time and have you eternally woven into the fabric of my life.

To the talented and creative Elin who illustrated the beautiful peonies that you see on the cover and throughout the interior of the book – thank you for being such a joy to work with and for taking my love for peonies and molding it into these special, one-of-a-kind creations.

And to my first true love, who's quirky, supportive, and lovable spirit inspired me to write and share what I considered to be my very first 'real' poem as an expression of my love for him at the tender age of 19. Little did I know at the time that my passion for writing was just beginning to ignite inside me.

About the Author

Michele Marie Neyers was raised amongst the cornfields in the land of 10,000 lakes, in her home state of Minnesota, and the windswept prairie lands of her adopted state of South Dakota. She graduated from South Dakota State University with degrees in mechanical engineering and engineering physics.

After spending 20+ years pursuing a successful career in education technology, she made a decision to shift her focus and energy towards her creative passions. She simply has a passion for creating beautiful things that are useful and useful things that are beautiful. Poetry and writing are that medium. Michele is the creator of *Juicy Conscious Living* and *1 Beautiful Thing* – additional writings, online teachings and programs she is bringing to a worldwide community – to support women of all ages to tune in to their inner wisdom and be the pioneers and designers of the lives they were always meant to lead.

Michele (along with her cat, Sophie) lives, works, kayaks, and writes near Annapolis, Maryland in a dream house she designed and built with breathtaking views of the water.

Connect with her online at www.micheleneyers.com and write to her at michele@micheleneyers.com.

3 Lines 30 Days Poetry Challenge Guidelines

INTRODUCTION

The *3 Lines 30 Days* poetry challenge is designed to be simple and available for everyone, adults and children alike. There are no complicated rules or fancy formats to follow. Honestly, there are only 2 simple things to remember: (1) Write 3 lines of poetry every day, and (2) Repeat for 30 continuous days.

WHAT YOU NEED

• A notebook or journal
• Colored pens/markers
• Your Imagination!

STEP 1 | TOOLS OF THE TRADE

Just like any task that you set before yourself, one of the primary considerations is to have the right tools for the job. Be sure to review the 'What You Need' list provided above. Grab a new journal or notebook that you already have on hand. If you don't have one on hand, take yourself on a little shopping date to find one that you absolutely love. One that inspires you just to look at it! While on your shopping excursion, pick up a new pen or two that feels good when you hold it between your fingers. One that glides across the paper easily and effortlessly. There simply is no substitute for a pen that can practically write the poems for you! A poor pen choice should never stand in the way of your ultimate creativity.

STEP 2 | BE ACCOUNTABLE + SHOW UP

This next step is perhaps the most important. Be totally committed. Choose the exact date that you will start the challenge. Determine ahead of time how you will stay accountable for each of the 30 days. It's longer than you think so plan ahead. This is what makes up a good challenge after all! What structures will you need to put in place to ensure that you fully show up for the challenge every day and get the most out of it? That might look like setting up a specific time on your calendar each day. Or setting a reminder on your smartphone. Maybe you want to ask a friend to do the challenge with you so you can be accountable to each other. Just be honest with yourself. Only you know what you need to put in place to ensure that you receive all the benefits a challenge like this has to offer.

STEP 3 | WRITE 3 LINES EVERY DAY

This is perhaps the simplest step of them all – write 3 lines every day. Notice that I said 'simple', not 'easy'. The challenge is intentionally designed to be simple. Anyone and everyone can write 3 lines. I promise. Where it becomes 'challenging' for some is when it comes to writing 3 lines every day for 30 continuous days (go back and read Step 2 again).

Even simpler is that the lines don't have to rhyme. They don't need to follow any particular format, like haiku. And a 'line' can be anything you decide it is. As you progress through the challenge, you will start to notice that inspiration can be found everywhere and anywhere. And you typically don't need to look far or wide for it. Sometimes it will be sitting right next to you. Or across the room. You may find it looking through a window or by staring at an object on your desk. Be open to receiving inspiration from the familiar and the unexpected places. And for those times when you need some added inspiration, I've created a list of 50 themes which you can choose from on the following pages.

STEP 4 | RINSE AND REPEAT FOR 30 DAYS

Now that you have the basic steps down, the only thing to do now is to 'rinse and repeat' for 30 continuous days. If doing the same thing every day for 30 days sounds a bit boring (or possibly even 'daunting') to you, remember that you have all the flexibility in the world to do things a little differently each day. Let yourself be inspired not only by what you write but how you go about the process. There is no 'right' way or 'one' way to do this challenge. Your creativity gets to have some fun with that as well.

Be sure to have fun. If the challenge begins to feel like more of a chore or burden, ask yourself 'How can I make this easy and fun?'. If you miss a day, whatever you do just don't quit! Get right back up on that horse and give yourself permission to begin again.

50 INSPIRATIONAL THEMES FOR YOUR
3 LINES POETRY CHALLENGE

1. FULL MOON
2. FAVORITE COLOR
3. SUMMER
4. ICED COFFEE
5. DARK CHOCOLATE
6. HEROES
7. HEROINES
8. TRAVEL
9. TROPICAL ISLAND
10. BELIEF
11. TREASURE
12. GRATITUDE
13. SUNSET
14. SUNRISE
15. BEAUTY
16. INNOCENCE
17. SIBLINGS
18. MUSIC
19. NATURE
20. MONEY
21. ABUNDANCE
22. SOUL MATE
23. CELEBRATION
24. PARTNERSHIP
25. PINK CONVERTIBLE

26. CHOPSTICKS
27. CANDLE
28. PURPLE
29. BOOKS
30. DONUTS
31. PEACHES
32. PEONIES
33. LOVE
34. PLEASURE
35. GUITAR
36. CALIFORNIA
37. SAILING
38. PEACE
39. FREEDOM
40. MUSE
41. PAINTBRUSHES
42. FAVORITE FOOD
43. FIRST LOVE
44. KISSES / KISSING
45. MERMAIDS
46. WINDCHIMES
47. SNOW
48. WINDOWS TO THE SOUL
49. HERITAGE
50. COMMUNITY

DAY 1

DAY 2

DAY 3

DAY 4

DAY 5

DAY 6

DAY 7

CONGRATULATIONS!

Way to GO! You DID it!

Congratulations on completing the first 7 days of the
3 Lines 30 Days Poetry Challenge.

What was your experience like?
Did you find that writing 3 lines each day came easily
or did you have some challenges?
If so, what were they?

Are you beginning to **hear** your inner poet?
What does his/her voice sound like?
Is there more than one voice?

Did you use the list of inspirational themes provided or
did you find other sources for your inspiration?
If so, what were they?

I'd love to hear about your experience and
introduce you to our
3 Lines 30 Days Poetry Challenge
online community. You can join us here:

www.facebook.com/groups/3lines30days

A Love Note For My Readers

H ello love!

First, please know how much it means to me that you are reading this love note from me right now. Living in this age of information and being surrounded (and let's face it – constantly barraged) by what we have at our fingertips, it really is a small miracle that we found one another. Then again, miracles are happening around us all the time. All we need to do is pay attention!

Second, if you loved this first book – and I certainly hope you did – please tell 745 of your closest friends and leave a review for me on Amazon. Not only would you be helping to move and inspire others through sharing poetry, but you would be allowing me to fulfill on one of my heart's deepest desires – to share my poetry and the poetry of others with as many people as I can.

Lastly, you can join me & other fans on my Facebook Fan Page and engage with me on Instagram. These are oftentimes the online places I share random poetry and other writings for the first time. For exclusive updates and news about upcoming books, giveaways, online programs and behind-the-scenes content, drop in your name and email address at www.micheleneyers.com. My team of poetry fairies will send you a little something special, along with our eternal gratitude.

May your heart and soul always be touched by poetry and all that is beautiful & lovely in the world.

With all my love, Michele

Let's Connect!

Website: www.micheleneyers.com
Blog: www.micheleneyers.com/journal
Facebook: www.facebook.com/AuthorMicheleMNeyers
Instagram: www.instagram.com/micheleneyers

THE LITERARY FAIRIES

We make your literary wish come true!

Michele Marie Neyers

has partnered with

The Literary Fairies

Their mission is to grant literary wishes to those who have experienced or are experiencing an adversity in their life or have a disability and wish to share their story with the world to uplift, inspire and entertain through literacy.

Visit TLF website now to find out how YOU could have your literary wish granted or if you wish to make a donation.

More details provided at
www.theliteraryfairies.com

.

www.ingramcontent.com/pod-product-compliance
Lightning Source LLC
Chambersburg PA
CBHW051431090426
42737CB00014B/2918